SPORTS CARS OF TOMORROW

BY MAE RESPICIO

CAPSTONE PRESS

a capstone imprint

Published by Spark, an imprint of Capstone
1710 Roe Crest Drive, North Mankato, Minnesota 56003
capstonepub.com

Library of Congress Cataloging-in-Publication Data
is available on the Library of Congress website.
ISBN: 9781669078944 (library binding)
ISBN: 9781669078890 (paperback)
ISBN: 9781669078906 (ebook PDF)

Summary: Sports cars grab people's attention wherever they go. What could these amazing cars look like in the future? How much faster could they go? With cutting-edge materials, automation, powerful electric engines, and more, sports car fans can look forward to many exciting new features. See what carmakers are planning for tomorrow's most thrilling sports cars!

Editorial Credits
Editors: Aaron Sautter and Carrie Sheely; Designer: Elyse White; Media Researcher: Svetlana Zhurkin; Production Specialist: Tori Abraham

Image Credits
Dreamstime: Max Earey, 20; Getty Images: -M-I-S-H-A-, cover (top right), Devrimb, cover (top left), Sjoerd van der Wal, 15, Viaframe, cover (bottom); Newscom: YNA/Yonhap News, 28; Shutterstock: Adam Kovacs, 12, Alexandros Michailidis, 18, Bascar, 1, 7, ben bryant, 8, Boykov, 23, Haggardous50000, 17, lassedesignen, 4, Marco Iacobucci Epp, 21, metamorworks, 11, Mike Mareen, 14, Mikhail Bakunovich, 5, North Monaco, 24, quiggyt4, 29, Steve Lagreca, 13, VanderWolf Images, 6, 26, 27, WinWin artlab (design element), cover and throughout, Zapp2Photo, 9

Printed and bound in the USA. 5853

CONTENTS

Words in **bold** are in the glossary.

THE FUTURE IS FASTER

Revving engines. Big wheels. Sleek bodies. All the parts of a sports car combine to make it stand out. What will these speedy cars be like in the future? What kinds of new **technology** will they have? And just how fast will they go? Let's take a peek into the world of tomorrow's sports cars!

Porsche Mission X concept car

Will sports cars of tomorrow still be fast? Yes! They'll have more powerful engines. They'll have automatic features. They'll be more **aerodynamic** to help them cut through the air.

All of these features will help sports cars go even faster than they already do. How do we know this? Carmakers build concept cars. These are models that show what future cars might do.

Aston Martin Vanquish Vision concept car

Today's technology will help designers build sports cars in the future. Imagine going down the road in a **luxurious** Lotus. But instead of driving, you sit back and relax. Why? There's no driver!

Lotus Eletre

Self-driving cars were once a dream of carmakers. Now, they're close to reality. Cars have cameras to see what's ahead and avoid dangers. They can speed up and slow down on their own.

Future sports cars will have high-tech heads-up displays (HUDs). Some might show 3D images called **holograms**. Pictures, words, and maps will appear on the windshield. The driver doesn't have to glance away to see information. This makes driving safer.

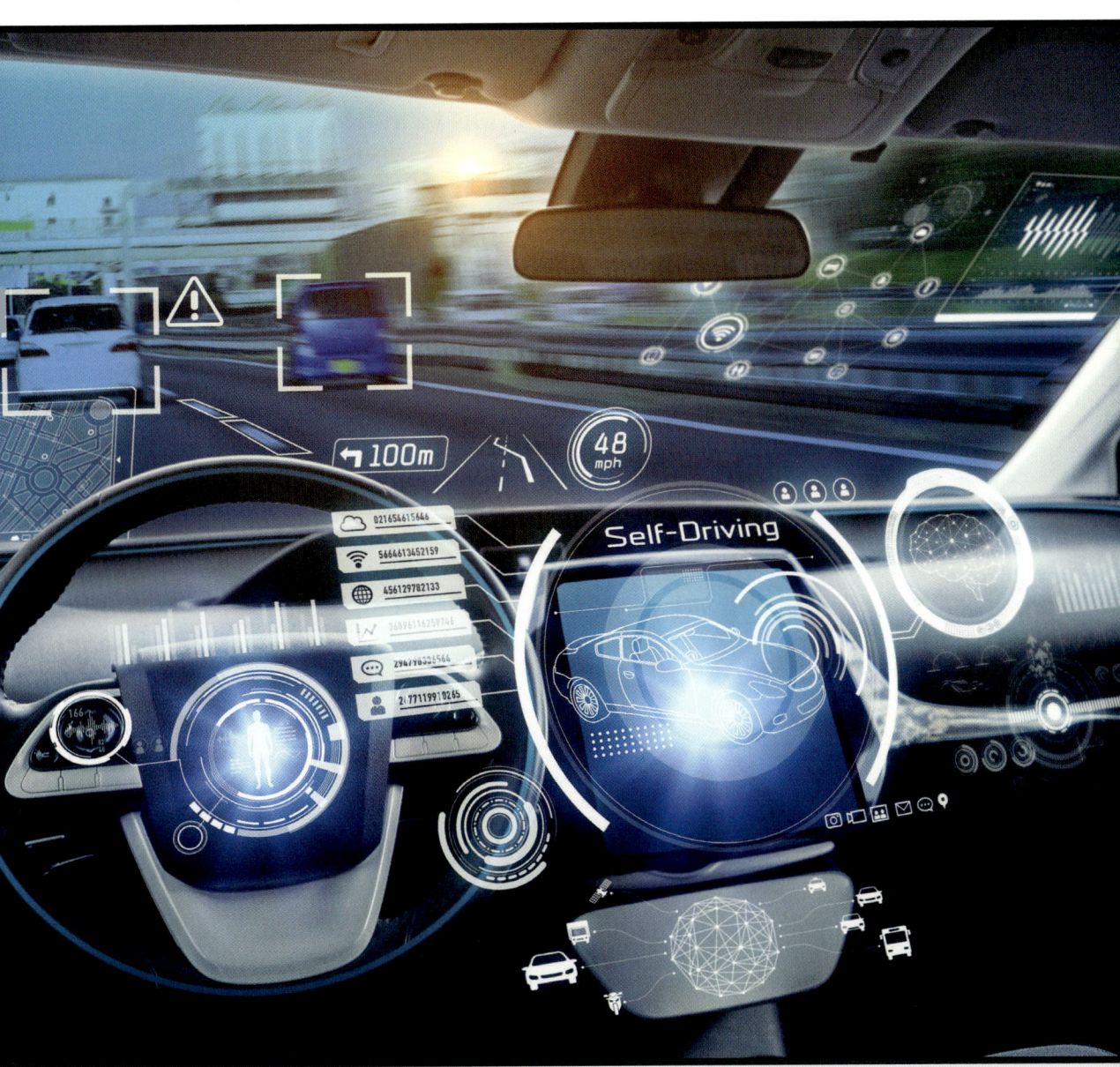

One of BMW's concept cars is called i Vision Dee. It can display digital scenes on the windshield. The driver can change what is shown by touching a slider. The car has a built-in voice assistant. The i Vision Dee's body can change between 32 colors.

BMW i Vision Dee

FACT

Nissan is working on technology for a car that
would understand signals from your brain.

ELECTRIC SPEED

Today, electric cars share roads with gas-powered cars. More sports cars are electric, such as the Maserati GranTurismo Folgore. The future will have more electric sports cars. They'll get better and faster.

Maserati GranTurismo Folgore

Maserati electric car platform

What makes electric cars special? Electric cars **accelerate** faster than gas-powered cars. When a driver steps on the accelerator pedal, the electric motor gives it instant power. *Zoom*!

Porsche's first all-electric sports car is the Taycan. It can go from 0 to 60 miles (97 kilometers) per hour in only 2.6 seconds!

Porsche Taycan

Teslas are known for their sleek body designs.

Tesla is a top electric carmaker. It is building the Roadster to be the fastest **production** car in the world. It would go from 0 to 60 miles (97 km) in only 1.9 seconds. Its top speed would be more than 250 miles (402 km) per hour.

Lotus Evija electric car

Electric sports cars are not just super speedy. They're better for the **environment**. Why? They cause less **pollution** than gas-powered cars.

Carmakers continue to improve electric cars. Some designers are trying to make them more lightweight. This can improve handling.

FACT

Electric cars race around the world in a series called Formula E.

FUTURISTIC FEATURES

Carmakers love trying new materials and features. They experiment with **carbon fiber**. It's light but strong. Carbon fiber makes cars faster. It's used for parts such as body panels and frames.

4C *Launch Edition*

The Alfa Romeo 4C has a carbon fiber frame.

Lamborghini LB744

Lamborghini built a new car. It's called the LB744. The carmaker built a new front frame for the car. It is all carbon fiber. The frame is sturdy. The car is light and quick.

FACT

Lamborghini and the Massachusetts Institute of Technology worked together to make a special car body with carbon fiber. When it is damaged, it can self-heal!

Carmakers find ways to make their cars more aerodynamic too. They make flaps that move to change how air flows around a car. They test new **spoilers** and **wings** for the back of the cars. The Porsche Taycan spent about 1,500 hours in a wind tunnel to test its aerodynamics.

wing

Porsche 911 GT2 RS

Porsche Taycan Turbo S

Do we know exactly how sports cars will be in the future? No. Still, we can imagine. We do know they'll be sleek and high-tech. And for sure they'll be super fast!

Porsche Vision 357 concept car

Corvette E-Ray

GLOSSARY

aerodynamic (air-oh-dye-NA-mik)—built to move easily through the air

carbon fiber (KAHR-buhn FY-buhr)—a strong, lightweight material used to make parts for vehicles

environment (in-VY-ruhn-muhnt)—the natural world of the land, water, and air

hologram (HOL-uh-gram)—an image made by laser beams that looks three-dimensional

luxurious (LUG-zhur-ee-us)—having something that is not needed but adds great ease and comfort

pollution (puh-LOO-shuhn)—materials that hurt Earth's water, air, and land

production (pruh-DUHK-shuhn)—describes a vehicle produced for mass-market sale

spoiler (SPOIL-uhr)—a part attached to the back of a car that helps improve the car's handling

technology (tek-NOL-uh-jee)—the use of science to do practical things, such as designing machines

wing (WING)—a long, flat panel on the back of a car

READ MORE

Chandler, Matt. *The Tech Behind Concept Cars*. North Mankato, MN: Capstone, 2020.

Klepeis, Alicia Z. *The Future of Transportation: From Electric Cars to Jet Packs*. North Mankato, MN: Capstone, 2020.

Rendle, Steve. *Sports Cars*. New York: PowerKids Press, 2022.

INTERNET SITES

An Electric Future
timeforkids.com/g56/an-electric-future-2

HowStuffWorks: How Sports Cars Work
auto.howstuffworks.com/sports-cars.htm

Lotus: Evija
lotuscars.com/en-US/evija

INDEX

ABOUT THE AUTHOR

Mae Respicio is a nonfiction writer and middle grade author. Her novel, *The House That Lou Built*, won an Asian Pacific American Libraries Association Honor Award and was an NPR Best Book. Mae has fun childhood memories of cruising around California with her dad in his 1968 classic Ford Mustang.